Kindle Empire Management Victory

Discover How To Manage Your Kindle EBook Empire, Increase Your Kindle EBook Sales And Prevent Your Kindle EBook Sales From Drying Up

Dominic. B. Frost

Dominicbfrost.com

Kindle Empire Management Victory   Dominic. B. Frost

Copyright © 2018 Dominic. B. Frost
All rights reserved.
ISBN-13: 978-1986282567
ISBN-10: 1986282562

COPYRIGHT

February 2018 Edition
Copyright © 2018 by Dominic. B. Frost All rights reserved.

No part of this book may be reproduced in any form or by any electronic or mechanical means including information storage and retrieval systems except in the case of brief quotations in articles or reviews - without the permission in writing from its publisher, Dominic. B. Frost.

DISCLAIMER

All brand names and products names used in this book are trademarks, or trade names or their respective holders. I am not associated with any product or vendor in this book.

The information provided herein is stated to be truthful and consistent, in that any liability, in terms of inattention or otherwise, by any usage or abuse of any policies, processes, or direction contained within is the solitary and utter responsibility of the recipient reader.

Under no circumstances will and legal responsibility or blame be held against the publisher and author for any reparation, damages, or monetary loss due to the information herein, either directly or indirectly.

Please note the information contained within this document is for educational and entertainment purposes only. Every attempt has been made to provide accurate, up to date and reliable, complete information. No warranties of any kind are expressed or implied. Readers acknowledge that the author is no engaging in the rendering of legal financial, medical or professional advice.

By reading this document, the reader agrees that under no circumstance are we responsible for any losses, direct or indirect which are incurred as a result of the use of information contained within this document, including but not limited to, -errors, omissions or inaccuracies.

TABLE OF CONTENT

INTRODUCTION ... 1

MANAGING YOUR KINDLE
EBOOK TITLES, SALES AND PROMOTIONAL DATES ... 3

BUNDLING YOUR KINDLE EBOOKS TOGETHER ... 12

ADD SOME OF YOUR KINDLE
EBOOKS TO OTHER MARKETPLACES ... 18

DECREASE THE PRICE
OF SOME OF YOUR KINDLE EBOOKS ... 23

PERMANENTLY GIVING
AWAY SOME OF YOUR KINDLE EBOOKS ... 26

GIVE AWAY SOME OF YOUR
KINDLE EBOOKS TO YOUR EMAIL SUBSCRIBERS ... 31

GIVE AWAY SOME OF YOUR
KINDLE EBOOKS ON YOUR WEBSITE ... 33

SUBMIT SOME OF YOUR FREE
KINDLE EBOOKS TO FORUMS WEBSITES AND MORE ... 34

CONCLUSION ... 35

INTRODUCTION

Firstly I'd like to say thank you for buying my Kindle Empire Management Victory book.

Within my Kindle Empire Management Victory book you will be firstly learning how you can easily manage the Kindle eBooks you've published.

You will then be learning a very simple trick which you can use to increase the amount of Kindle eBooks you've published without having to write a single word which can increase your Kindle eBook sales.

Finally you will learning some of the strategies you can use to reverse, stop or stall the dry up of Kindle eBook sales.

These strategies should not be used with all the Kindle eBooks you've published and should only be used as a last resort because you'll be unable to have access to certain perks such as the KDP Select enrolment, the 70% royalty fee for each Kindle eBook sold and so on.

However if your Kindle eBook sales are decreasing despite your marketing and promotional efforts then using some of these techniques may help either reverse, stop or stall the decrease of your Kindle eBook sales.

I hope you enjoy reading my Kindle Empire Management Victory book and once again thank you buying my book.

Dominic. B. Frost

Dominicbfrost.com

Facebook: https://www.facebook.com/Dominic-B-Frost-1486663614766022/

Twitter: https://twitter.com/DominicBFrost

MANAGING YOUR KINDLE EBOOK TITLES, SALES AND PROMOTIONAL DATES

Managing your Kindle eBook titles, sales and promotional dates is important because you need to know the following.

- Which Kindle eBooks are selling well.
- Which Kindle eBooks aren't selling well.
- When you can begin your Kindle eBook promotions.
- How many promotional days you have left to promote your Kindle eBooks.

To do this you should log the following information down within a spreadsheet document when you publish your Kindle eBooks.

- Your Kindle eBook titles.
- Your Kindle eBook author/pen names.
- Your Kindle eBook description.
- Your KDP Select enrolment term start and end dates.
- Your free Kindle eBook promotion start and end dates.
- How many free Kindle eBooks were downloaded.
- Your Kindle countdown promotion start and end dates.
- The price of your Kindle eBook when you run a Kindle Countdown promotion.
- The amount of sales your Kindle eBook receives when you run a Kindle Countdown promotion.

You should also create another spreadsheet document/sheet where you log the following information.

- Your Kindle eBook titles.
- Your Kindle eBook author/pen names.

- The price your charging for each of your Kindle eBooks sold.
- How much commission you earn for the sale of each of your Kindle eBooks.
- Your Kindle eBook daily, monthly and yearly sales/profits.
- Your Paperback and Audiobook daily, monthly and yearly sales/profits.
- Which Kindle eBooks are being read from the Kindle Unlimited and the Kindle Owners' Lending Library.
- How many pages are being read from the Kindle Unlimited and from the Kindle Owners' Lending Library on a daily, weekly, monthly and yearly basis.

Why Do I Need To Use A Spreadsheet File To Log This Information?

You will need to use a spreadsheet file to log this information so that you can easily sort the dates of your Kindle eBook promotions, your Kindle eBook sale figures and other dates/figures in ascendingly and descending order.

Why Do I Need To Separate The Information Within Two Spreadsheet Files/Sheets?

Adding the marketing, sales and profit information altogether within one file/sheet can be confusing.

However if you separate the information into two different files/sheets then you can manage and organise the information more clearly and easily.

Where Can I Find This Information?

Most of the information such as Kindle eBook titles, author/pen name and description you will already have available to you.

However information on your KDP Select dates, promotions, Kindle eBook sales and the amount of pages read can be found within the bookshelf, reports and the promotion and advertising sections of your KDP accounts at https://kdp.amazon.com.

You can also find your Paperback and Audiobook sales within your other accounts you've opened.

Why Do I Need To Log The Kindle EBook Titles, Author/Pen Names, Description?

You need to log information about your Kindle eBooks so you know which Kindle eBooks need marketing, what author/pen name you've used for your Kindle eBook and what your Kindle eBooks are about.

Why Should I Log My KDP Select Enrolment Dates?

Your KDP Select enrolment dates for each Kindle eBook expires after ninety days of enrolment after which the enrolment should automatically renew itself and you'll be able to rerun your free Kindle promotion and Kindle Countdown deals.

This will mean you can start marketing your Kindle eBooks again which will increase your Kindle eBook popularity and will increase your Kindle eBook sales.

Which is why adding the KDP Select start and end dates and sorting the dates in ascending and descending order is important.

However you need to make sure that your KDP Select enrolment for each Kindle eBook you've published are renewed before ninety days expiry date by doing the following.

1. Visit your Kindle Bookshelf within https://kdp.amazon.com.

2. Find the Kindle eBook which is about to expire and click the promote and advertise button.
3. Check and log the dates within the KDP Select section.
4. Click onto the Manage KDP Select enrolment button.
5. If the radio button hasn't been checked then click onto the radio button to ensure your Kindle Select enrolment will be renewed.

How Do I Stop The Renewal Of My Kindle EBooks From The KDP Select Program?

Details on how to stop the renewal of your Kindle eBooks from the KDP Select program are available within the renewal section of the following website https://kdp.amazon.com/en_US/help/topic/G201541150.

Isn't There Any Way I Can Immediately Stop My Kindle EBooks From Being Enrolled Into The KDP Select Program?

If your Kindle eBooks have only been enrolled or renewed within the last three days then you can cancel your KDP Select enrolment by following the cancellation steps within the following website https://kdp.amazon.com/en_US/help/topic/G201541150.

If however your Kindle eBooks have been enrolled onto the KDP Select program for longer than three days then unfortunately you will have to wait until the KDP Select program expires in ninety days' time.

Can't I Violate The KDP Select Program And Make My Kindle EBooks Available Within Other Marketplaces Immediately?

If you violate the KDP Select program then any royalties you've earned from the sale of your Kindle eBooks over the ninety day period will not be paid.

You'll also risk having all your Kindle eBooks being removed from the KDP Select program and being blocked from using the KDP Select program.

This will mean you will no longer be able to run a free Kindle promotion or a Kindle Countdown deal on any of your Kindle eBooks and people will no longer be able to read any of your Kindle eBooks through the Kindle Unlimited and Kindle Owners' Lending Library.

This will affect your Kindle eBook marketing, sales and profits which is why you should never violate the KDP Select program.

Why Do I Need To Log The Free Kindle EBook Promotion Start And End Dates?

You need to log the free Kindle promotion start and end dates so you'll when know your Kindle eBooks will be free for people to download and you can prepare to market your Kindle eBooks before and during the free promotion dates.

Why Do I Need To Log How Many Kindle EBooks Have Been Downloaded From My Free Kindle Promotion?

You need to log how many of your Kindle eBooks were downloaded from your free Kindle promotion in order to see how effective this form of marketing is and to see if the number of free downloaded decreases over time.

Why Do I Need To Log The Kindle Countdown Promotion Start And End Dates?

You need to log the Kindle Countdown promotion start and end dates so that you can prepare to increase your marketing campaign before and during the Kindle Countdown promotion dates.

Why Do I Need To Log Kindle EBook Price And Sales When I Run A Kindle Countdown Promotion?

You need to log the price and sales of your Kindle eBooks when you run a Kindle Countdown promotion in order to see whether the price of your Kindle eBook increases/decrease the amount of Kindle eBook sales.

This will help you decide whether or not the price of some of your Kindle eBooks should be permanently decreased.

Why Do I Need To Log The Price Of My Kindle EBooks?

You need to log how much you're charging your readers to buy your Kindle eBooks so that you can see whether or not an increase/decrease in sales is due to the price of your Kindle eBooks.

Why Do I Need To Log How Much Commission I Earn For The Sale Of Each Of My Kindle EBooks?

You need to log how much commission you earn for the sale of each of your Kindle eBooks so that you can see how much you will earn from each Kindle eBook being sold.

The commission may vary if you're selling within other marketplaces so you may need to use multiple rows within your spreadsheet.

Why Do I Need To Log My Daily, Monthly And Yearly Sales/Profits?

You need to log your daily, monthly and yearly sales/profits so that you can see the increasing or decreasing in sales/profits over a given period of time.

This includes logging the sales of your Paperback Books and Audiobooks.

Why Do I Need To Log Which Kindle EBooks Are Being Read From The Kindle Unlimited And The Kindle Owners' Lending Library?

You need to log which Kindle eBooks are being read so that you know that you're not only making money from your Kindle eBook sales but you're also making money from the people reading your Kindle eBooks from the Kindle Unlimited and the Kindle Owners' Lending Library.

Why Do I Need To Log How Many Pages Of My Kindle EBooks Are Being Read From The Kindle Unlimited And The Kindle Owners' Lending Library On A Daily, Weekly, Monthly And Yearly Basis?

You need to log how many pages your Kindle eBooks are being read on a daily, weekly, monthly and yearly basis so that you can see which Kindle eBooks are more profitable than others and whether there is an increase/decrease in pages being read over a given period of time.

Are There Any Tools Which Can Help Me Manage My Kindle EBooks?

There is a tool called Koptimizer 2.0 which I have reviewed on my website at http://dominicbfrost.com/koptimzer-2-0-review/.

Koptimizer 2.0 will not only help you manage your Kindle eBooks but it will also help you track sales, keywords and much more.

Is There Anything Else I Should Log?

You'll need log your marketing efforts and the sales of your other products/services your either promoting or selling on your website within another spreadsheet file/sheet.

What Information Should I Log Within My Marketing Spreadsheet File/Sheet?

Unfortunately I cannot tell you what marketing information to log within the spreadsheet file/sheet as everyone will be using different marketing methods.

But it's essential that all of your marketing efforts are logged so you do not make any errors such as submitting your Kindle eBooks to websites you've already submitted to, marketing the wrong Kindle eBooks and so on.

What Information Should I Log Within The Other Products/Services Sales Spreadsheet File/Sheet?

The type of information you should be logging about the other products/services your either selling or promoting on your website are as follows.

- Title of product/services.
- Are you selling or promoting the product/service.
- Are you receiving a one off payment or recurring payments for the sale of the products/services.
- Commission rate.
- Amount of daily, weekly, monthly and yearly sales and profits.

Is There Anything Else I Should Do?

You should check your promotional dates regularly so that you know when you can start another Kindle eBook promotion.

You should use a web analytic service such as Google Analytics or Statcounter for your website so that you can keep track of how many people are visiting your website, where your website visitors are coming from, what website pages are popular and so on.

Finally and most importantly you should keep track of your Kindle eBook, Paperback and Audiobook sales and performance.

BUNDLING YOUR KINDLE EBOOKS TOGETHER

Bundling your Kindle eBooks together is an excellent way to increase your Kindle eBook sales.

It's also a great way to significantly increase the amount of Kindle eBooks you've published.

How Will Bundling My Kindle EBooks Together Significantly Increase the Amount of Kindle EBooks I've Published?

There are different ways you can bundle your Kindle eBooks.

For instance if you've published four Kindle eBooks together then you can bundle your Kindle eBooks in the following way.

1. Bundle all four Kindle eBooks together.
2. Bundle the first three Kindle eBooks together.
3. Bundle the last three Kindle eBooks together.
4. Bundle the first two Kindle eBooks together.
5. Bundle the last two Kindle eBooks together.
6. Bundle the middle two Kindle eBooks together.
7. Mix your Kindle eBook bundles together (shouldn't be done with fictional Kindle eBooks).

This can increase your four Kindle eBooks into fifteen Kindle eBooks.

Why Can't I Mix My Fictional Kindle EBooks Together?

If you have created different storylines for each fictional Kindle eBook you've published then you can mix your fictional Kindle eBooks together.

However if your storyline continues throughout your entire Kindle eBook series then bundling and mixing your Kindle eBooks together will leave plot holes and gaps.

For instance if you bundle Kindle eBooks one and four together then the people who read your bundled Kindle eBooks will be confused when they start reading your fourth Kindle eBook because they didn't read your second and third Kindle eBooks.

When Should I Bundle My Kindle EBooks Together?

You should look at bundling your Kindle eBooks immediately as this can increase the amount of sales you make from your Kindle eBooks.

How Much Should I Charge My Readers To Buy My Bundled Kindle EBooks?

I recommend you charge your readers more than the usual $2.99 for your bundled Kindle eBooks because you are selling more than just one Kindle eBook.

But you want to provide your readers with a bargain for buying two to four Kindle eBooks together rather than just buying the one Kindle eBook.

So I would recommend you charge an extra $1.00 to $2.00 for each Kindle eBook you bundle together.

However it's completely up to you how you want to price your Kindle eBooks.

Should My Bundled Kindle EBooks Be Part Of The KDP Select Program?

The KDP Select exclusivity agreement states that no part of the digital version of your Kindle eBooks can be sold within other marketplaces and only 10% of your Kindle eBooks can be given away as a sample.

So if your Kindle eBooks are part of the KDP Select program then your bundled Kindle eBooks can only be sold within Amazon and nowhere else which is why I recommend you enrol your bundled Kindle eBooks within the KDP Select program.

However if your Kindle eBooks are not part of the KDP Select program and are available to buy within other marketplaces then your bundled Kindle eBooks cannot be part of the KDP Select program.

I Want to Sell My Kindle EBooks and Bundled Kindle EBooks within Other Marketplace but they're All Part of the KDP Select Program What Should I Do?

You will firstly have to stop the renewal of both your Kindle eBooks and your bundled Kindle eBooks from the KDP Select program.

Details on how to do this are available within the renewal section of the following website
https://kdp.amazon.com/en_US/help/topic/G201541150.

You'll then unfortunately have to wait until the KDP Select program on both your Kindle eBooks and your bundled Kindle eBooks expires before selling them within other marketplaces.

This can be tricky if you enrolled your Kindle eBooks and your bundled Kindle eBooks into the KDP Select program at different dates as you could be waiting for up to six months before they're all no longer enrolled onto the KDP Select program.

Should I Run A Free Kindle Promotion On My

Bundled Kindle EBooks?

You can technically run a free Kindle Promotion on all your bundled Kindle eBooks as long as your bundled Kindle eBooks are enrolled in the KDP Select program.

However in my opinion it would be better to wait until you've published more Kindle eBooks and the sales of your Kindle eBooks starts to dry up before you run a free Kindle eBook promotion on your bundled Kindle eBooks.

This will ensure that you maximize your Kindle eBook sales and profits.

I also recommend that you start with the two to three Kindle eBook bundles when you are ready to begin the free Kindle promotion.

This will hopefully tempt the people who are downloading your free bundled Kindle eBooks into buying some of your other Kindle eBooks.

Should I Run A Kindle Countdown Deal On My Bundled Kindle EBooks?

This is the best marketing method you can use to promote your bundled Kindle eBooks as your Kindle eBook readers will be getting a great discount which is time sensitive plus they will be getting more than just one Kindle eBook.

However I recommend you only make your two to three Kindle eBook bundles as part of your Kindle Countdown deal which will hopefully tempt your Kindle eBook readers into buying some of your other published Kindle eBooks.

Should I Bundle My Paperback And Audiobooks Together?

If you have bundled your Kindle eBooks together then you should bundle your Paperback books together as well.

However Audiobooks can be a challenge when it comes to bundling them together.

In my opinion you should focus on bundling Your Kindle and Paperback books and consider bundling your Audiobooks later on when you have some free time available.

What Problems May Occur When Bundling My Kindle EBooks?

The first problem you may encounter is waiting for your KDP Select enrolment to expire on both you Kindle eBook and bundled Kindle eBooks if you want to sell them within other marketplaces.

The second problem you may encounter is the file size of your bundled Kindle eBooks can be too big to upload onto your KDP account.

This usually isn't a problem with non-fictional Kindle eBooks as they're usually twenty five to seventy five pages long which won't take up too much memory when bundled together.

However if your publishing full length fictional Kindle eBooks with a lot of pages or your Kindle eBook has a lot of images then the file size maybe too big to upload within your KDP account.

The third and final problem you may encounter is creating a new cover for your bundled Kindle eBooks.

This problem however is easily resolved by taking the covers of your Kindle eBooks and somehow merging them together.

Can I Bundle Two Different Kindle EBook Series Together?

You can technically bundle two Kindle eBook series together.

However your bundled Kindle eBooks file size maybe too large to upload onto your KDP accounts.

You're also unlikely to get readers interested in buying your bundled Kindle eBooks if you bundle two different storylines or topics together.

This is why I recommend you do not do this unless the file size isn't too large to upload onto your KDP accounts and the Kindle eBooks series are within a similar topic or storyline.

ADD SOME OF YOUR KINDLE EBOOKS TO OTHER MARKETPLACES

Adding some of your Kindle eBooks to other marketplaces is another technique you can use to gain more sales.

However before you do this you will need to select the Kindle eBooks you want to add within other marketplaces carefully as you will need to stop them from being renewed onto the KDP Select enrolment and you'll have to wait until your enrolment expires before selling them within other marketplaces.

You'll also be unable to run any free Kindle promotion and Kindle Countdown promotions on your chosen Kindle eBooks and people will be unable to read them within their Kindle Unlimited subscription and the Kindle Owners' Lending Library.

So Why Should I Consider Adding Some My Kindle EBooks To Other Marketplaces?

Adding your Kindle eBooks within other marketplaces can increase your Kindle eBook sales because your Kindle eBooks will be more widely available which can increase your Kindle eBook exposure online.

You may also benefit from a better commission rate by adding your Kindle eBook within other marketplaces.

When Should I Consider Adding Some Of My Kindle EBooks Within Other Marketplaces?

It's all comes down to how long your Kindle eBooks are not being sold and read and the amount of Kindle eBooks you have published.

For instance if you have a hundred of Kindle eBooks which are each being bought once a month and are also being read once a month then although you are then you're making $299 a month.

You're also making money from people who are reading your Kindle eBooks each month so you could be making around $350 to $400 a month passive income which is enough of a reason not to add your Kindle eBooks within other marketplaces.

If however you notice a few Kindle eBooks which have not been sold or read for over nine months and you have exhausted your marketing and promotional efforts then you should look at adding your Kindle eBooks within other marketplaces.

What Are The Best Kindle EBooks To Add Within Other Marketplaces?

If you're published a series of fictional Kindle eBooks which are have not been sold or read for a long period of time then it's best to add the first Kindle eBook within your Kindle eBook series to other marketplaces and leave the rest within the KDP Select program.

This will hopefully increase the sale of your first fictional Kindle eBook and the sales/readers of your other Kindle eBooks within the KDP Select program.

If however you have published non-fictional Kindle eBooks then I would focus on adding your least performing Kindle eBooks onto the other marketplaces.

What Should I Do Before I Add My Kindle EBooks Within Other Marketplaces?

You will firstly need to stop the renewal of your chosen Kindle eBooks within the KDP Select program.

Details on how to do this are available within the renewal section of the following website https://kdp.amazon.com/en_US/help/topic/G201541150.

You'll then need to wait until the KDP Select enrolment expires which can take up to ninety days.

What Marketplaces Can I Add My Kindle EBooks To?

I have a selection of marketplaces you can use to add your Kindle eBooks to on my website at http://dominicbfrost.com/alternative-kindle-ebook-marketplaces/.

What Else Will I Need To Do If I Decide To Add Some Of My Kindle EBooks Within Other Marketplaces?

You'll need to do the following.

1. Setup an account within the other marketplaces.
2. Change the file type and format of your Kindle eBooks.
3. Add your Kindle eBook details.
4. Upload your Kindle eBook within the other marketplaces.
5. Decide and add the price of your Kindle eBooks.
6. Publish your Kindle eBooks onto the marketplace.

Should I Consider Adding All Of My Kindle EBooks Within Other Marketplaces?

If your Kindle eBook sales have increased significantly within other marketplaces and your other Kindle eBook sales and readers within the KDP Select program are not improving then adding some of your other Kindle eBooks within these marketplaces maybe beneficial.

However if you do this then you will have to stop the renewal of your KDP enrolment and wait until the KDP expires which can take up to ninety days.

Your Kindle eBooks will also no longer have any access to the KDP Select promotional tools and people will no longer be able to read your Kindle eBooks through their Kindle Unlimited subscription and the Kindle Owners' Lending Library.

In my opinion it would be best if you add each Kindle eBook within your Kindle eBook collection slowly over a given period of time and see whether your other Kindle eBooks sales and readers within the KDP Select program increases.

If there's no improvement then you should look at adding more Kindle eBooks within other marketplace when the KDP Select enrolment expires.

If however there is an improvement then I would leave your other Kindle eBooks within the KDP Select program until your sales and readers decline again.

However the decision on what Kindle eBooks to add within other marketplaces is completely up to you.

What Should I Do If My Kindle EBooks Do Not Improve Despite Adding Them Within Other Marketplaces?

If your Kindle eBook sales don't increase despite being available within other marketplaces then your will need to look at reading the Decrease The Price Of Some Of Your Kindle Ebooks and the Permanently Giving Away Some Of Your Kindle Ebooks of book.

Can I Enrol My Kindle EBooks To The KDP Select Exclusivity Program Again?

You are allowed to enrol your Kindle eBooks within the KDP Select exclusivity program again as long as you remove your Kindle eBooks from the other marketplaces.

DECREASE THE PRICE OF SOME OF YOUR KINDLE EBOOKS

Decreasing the price of your Kindle eBooks is another method you can use to increase your Kindle eBook sales as people are always keen for a bargain.

However if you decrease your Kindle eBooks lower than $2.99 then you will run into the following problems.

1. The commission rate you will receive from the sale of your Kindle eBooks will fall from 70% to 35%.
2. You'll be ineligible for the Kindle Countdown promotion.

You may also find that a decrease in price of your Kindle eBook price does not necessarily guarantee an increase in Kindle eBook sales and any increase in will likely be temporary.

When Should I Decreasing The Price Of My Kindle EBooks?

In my opinion you should not decrease the price of your Kindle eBooks unless the following criteria is met.

1. You haven't got any sales of your Kindle eBooks within the last three to nine months.
2. You've exhausted your marketing efforts through the use of free Kindle promotional days and Kindle Countdown deals.

When the criteria is met then you'll need to see whether people are still reading your Kindle eBooks through the Kindle Unlimited subscription and through the Kindle Owners' Lending Library.

If people are reading your Kindle eBooks through the Kindle Unlimited subscription and through the Kindle Owners' Lending

Library or the Kindle eBook sales within other marketplaces decreases then you should look at decreasing the price of your Kindle eBooks.

If however people aren't reading your Kindle eBooks through the Kindle Unlimited subscription and through the Kindle Owners' Lending Library then you should consider adding your Kindle eBooks to other marketplaces before decreasing the price of your Kindle eBooks as this may increase your Kindle eBook sales.

More details on how to add your Kindle eBook within other marketplaces can be found in the previous chapter of book.

Why Shouldn't I Add My Kindle EBook Within Other Marketplaces If People Are Reading My Kindle EBooks Through The Kindle Unlimited Subscription And The Kindle Owners' Lending Library?

If you sell your Kindle eBooks within other marketplaces then your Kindle eBooks can no longer be part of the KDP exclusivity program which means people can no longer read your Kindle eBooks through their Kindle Unlimited subscription and through the Kindle Owners' Lending Library.

This means that you will lose the passive income you're making from the people who are reading your Kindle eBooks rather than buying them.

You'll also know that people are keen to read your Kindle eBooks rather than buy them because the price of your Kindle eBooks is too high.

So the best approach if you have a lot of readers of your Kindle eBooks through the Kindle Unlimited subscription and the Kindle

Owners' Lending Library is to reduce the price of your Kindle eBooks.

Should I Decrease My Kindle EBooks Lower Than $2.99?

You should try your best to avoid pricing your Kindle eBooks lower than $2.99 so that you can keep the 70% commission structure.

However if your making barely any sales of some of your Kindle eBooks despite it being priced at $2.99 then it's probably best to reduce the price below the $2.99 threshold and receive the 35% commission instead of the 70% commission.

PERMANENTLY GIVING AWAY SOME OF YOUR KINDLE EBOOKS

Permanently giving away some of your Kindle eBooks is another way you can use to increase your Kindle eBook sales as you'll be able to use your permanently free Kindle eBooks to market your other Kindle eBooks in your collection which can increase your Kindle eBook sales.

You'll also notice that people will be keen to download and possibly read your permanently free Kindle eBooks as people are always looking for something for free on the internet.

However you should only take this step with your Kindle eBooks if the following criteria are met.

1. You've exhausted your Kindle eBooks marketing and promotional efforts.
2. You've decreased the price of your Kindle eBooks to $0.99.
3. Your Kindle eBooks have not been sold and read on Amazon for over six to nine months.
4. Your Kindle eBooks are no longer part of the KDP Select program.
5. You're Kindle eBooks are not selling within other marketplaces.
6. The Paperback and audio versions of your Kindle eBooks are no longer selling.

Should I Make All The Kindle EBooks Which Have Met The Criteria Permanently Free?

You should make a few of your Kindle eBooks which have met the criteria permanently free and keep some of your other Kindle eBooks for sale.

You should then use the permanently free Kindle eBooks to market your other Kindle eBooks which have met the criteria but are still on sale.

This will hopefully reverse the dry up of sales of some of your Kindle eBooks which have met the criteria.

However if there is no change in sales then making all of your Kindle eBooks which have met the criteria permanently free and you should use them to market the Kindle eBooks which are selling well.

What Kindle EBooks Should I Start Making Permanently Free?

If you've published a series of non-fictional Kindle eBooks then you should make your least sold and read Kindle eBooks permanently free first.

If however you're publishing a series of fictional Kindle eBooks within the same storyline then you should only make your first Kindle eBook within the series permanently free and use it to market the other fictional Kindle eBooks within the series.

Should I Consider Creating and Publishing a Permanently Free Kindle eBook To Market My Other Kindle EBooks?

Creating and publishing a very short twenty five to fifty page permanently free fictional Kindle eBook is a great way to market and promote your full length Kindle eBooks as long as the storyline is based in some way with your full length fictional Kindle eBooks.

However if you're publishing non-fictional Kindle eBooks then I wouldn't use this method as your main focus should be to publishing and selling short non-fictional Kindle eBooks not giving them away.

What Should I Do Before I Make My Kindle EBooks Permanently Free?

You should make sure your other books chapter is marketing the Kindle eBooks you want to promote and you should make sure your website and social media accounts are also being marketed within your Kindle eBooks.

Why Shouldn't I Make My Kindle EBooks Permanently Free If The Paperback And Audio Versions Of My Kindle EBooks Are Still Selling?

You should not make your Kindle eBooks permanently free if the Paperback and audio versions of your Kindle eBooks are still selling well because it may result in less Paperback and audio versions of your Kindle eBook being sold.

How Do I Make My Kindle EBooks On Amazon Permanently Free?

Firstly you will need to make your Kindle eBooks within other marketplaces available to download for free.

You'll then need to get your friends, family members and Kindle eBook reader to go to your Kindle eBook web pages and report to Amazon that your Kindle eBooks are free within other marketplaces.

This will hopefully convince Amazon to make your Kindle eBooks permanently free.

However it can take a few weeks or months before Amazon decides whether or not to do this.

Until then you will have to keep checking your Kindle web page and market your permanently free Kindle eBooks within other marketplaces.

Why Can't I Report My Kindle EBooks Being Free Myself?

You can't report your Kindle eBooks being free yourself because Amazon is looking for readers to report your Kindle eBooks being free and if you report it yourself then there is a bigger chance that Amazon will not make your Kindle eBooks permanently free.

Is There Anything I Can Do To Convince Amazon To Make My Kindle EBooks Permanently Free?

The only way you can increase your chances of making your Kindle eBooks permanently free by getting more people to report that your Kindle eBook is free within other marketplaces.

What Should I Do If Amazon Hasn't Made My Kindle EBooks Permanently Free After A Few Months?

If Amazon hasn't made your Kindle eBooks permanently free after a few months then you should continue to focus your attention on marketing your permanently free Kindle eBooks within other marketplaces as its unlikely Amazon is going to make your Kindle eBooks permanently free.

You may not get as many downloads as you would do if your Kindle eBooks are available for free on Amazon but you will still get a lot.

Where Can I Market My Permanently Free Kindle EBooks?

You can market your permanently free Kindle eBooks within your social media accounts, the free Kindle eBook promotional websites and the forums you've joined

You can also do a simple search for free giveaway forums/website within Google and try and market your permanently free Kindle eBooks from there.

More details on how to market your Kindle eBooks can be found within my [Kindle Marketing Victory](#) book.

GIVE AWAY SOME OF YOUR KINDLE EBOOKS TO YOUR EMAIL SUBSCRIBERS

Giving away your Kindle eBooks to your email subscribers is an excellent way to increase your email subscriber list and keep your current email subscribers happy.

You'll also be able to use your free Kindle eBooks you're giving to your email subscribers to promote your other Kindle eBooks.

How Do I Make My Free Kindle EBooks Available To Download To My Email Subscribers?

You will firstly need to convert your free Kindle eBook into a PDF format.

You'll then need to upload your Kindle eBook onto your website and setup a web page where people can visit and click onto a website link to download their free PDF Kindle eBooks.

Finally you will need to send a broadcast message to your current subscribers letting them know they can download your Kindle eBooks for free by visiting a web page, click onto a download link and selecting where they want to save their Kindle eBooks.

What Else Should I Do?

You should change the first scheduled message so that your new subscribers will be able to download your free Kindle eBook by visiting a web page, clicking onto a download link and selecting where they want to save their Kindle eBooks.

You should also let your website visitors know that they'll receive a free PDF copy of your Kindle eBook when they subscribe to your newsletter.

GIVE AWAY SOME OF YOUR KINDLE EBOOKS ON YOUR WEBSITE

If your Kindle eBook sales and downloads are decreasing despite it being free on Amazon, other marketplaces and to all your email subscribers then offering your Kindle eBooks to your website visitors is the next method you should use.

Your free Kindle eBooks will be available to anyone who visits your website and will not require them to subscribe to your email newsletter.

How Do I Make My Kindle EBook Available To My Website Visitors?

All you have to do to offer your website visitors your free Kindle eBook is add a link within your website homepage or post where they can download your Kindle eBooks for free.

What Should I Do Before I Make My Kindle EBooks Available To All My Website Visitors?

You should make sure your other books chapter is marketing the Kindle eBooks you want to promote and you should make sure your website and social media accounts are also being marketed within your free Kindle eBooks.

SUBMIT SOME OF YOUR FREE KINDLE EBOOKS TO FORUMS WEBSITES AND MORE

If you are giving away your Kindle eBooks on your website then you might as well submit your free Kindle eBooks to forums, eBook/document sharing websites, website owners, and social media websites.

How Do I Find Websites That I Can Use To Submit My Free Kindle EBook To?

You can do a simple search on a search engine for websites/forums within your Kindle eBooks genre or topic.

You'll then need to visit each of the websites you've found, find out how to contact the website owner and see if they're interested in making your Kindle eBooks available to download on their website for free.

You should also upload your Kindle eBook to file/document sharing sites which I've listed at http://dominicbfrost.com/document-file-sharing-websites/ and you should search for and post your free Kindle eBook pdf/web links to freebie forums, directory listings and websites.

What Else Should I Do?

You should make sure your free Kindle eBooks are marketing your website, social media accounts and other Kindle eBooks you're selling.

CONCLUSION

Everyone who has read this book should consider using the first two strategies in helping you manage and increase the amount of Kindle eBooks you've published.

However the other strategies should only be used if your Kindle eBook sales and readers are decreasing over a long period of time.

Hopefully you will not need to use the other strategies and your Kindle eBooks will continue to make regular sales which will continue to make you a passive income.

But if you do need to use these strategies then you need to select the Kindle eBooks you want to use for these strategies carefully.

However if you still cannot stop the decrease in Kindle eBook sales despite you using the all the strategies within this book then unfortunately there is nothing you can do except create and publish a new series of Kindle eBooks which will help you increase and maintain your passive income.

THANK YOU

Finally I'd like to say thank you for downloading my book.

If you enjoyed reading my book then I'd really appreciate it if you would post a short review on Amazon by visiting the link below.

https://www.amazon.com/dp/B07B7NX43W

Also please check out my other Kindle and Paperback books available within the following pages and check out my websites at http://dominicbfrost.com/ for more information and updates.

Dominic. B. Frost

http://dominicbfrost.com/

Facebook: https://www.facebook.com/Dominic-B-Frost-1486663614766022/

Twitter: https://twitter.com/DominicBFrost

OTHER BOOKS

Available To Buy From Amazon At
 https://www.amazon.com/dp/B07B7NKS67
Get Your Copy Now

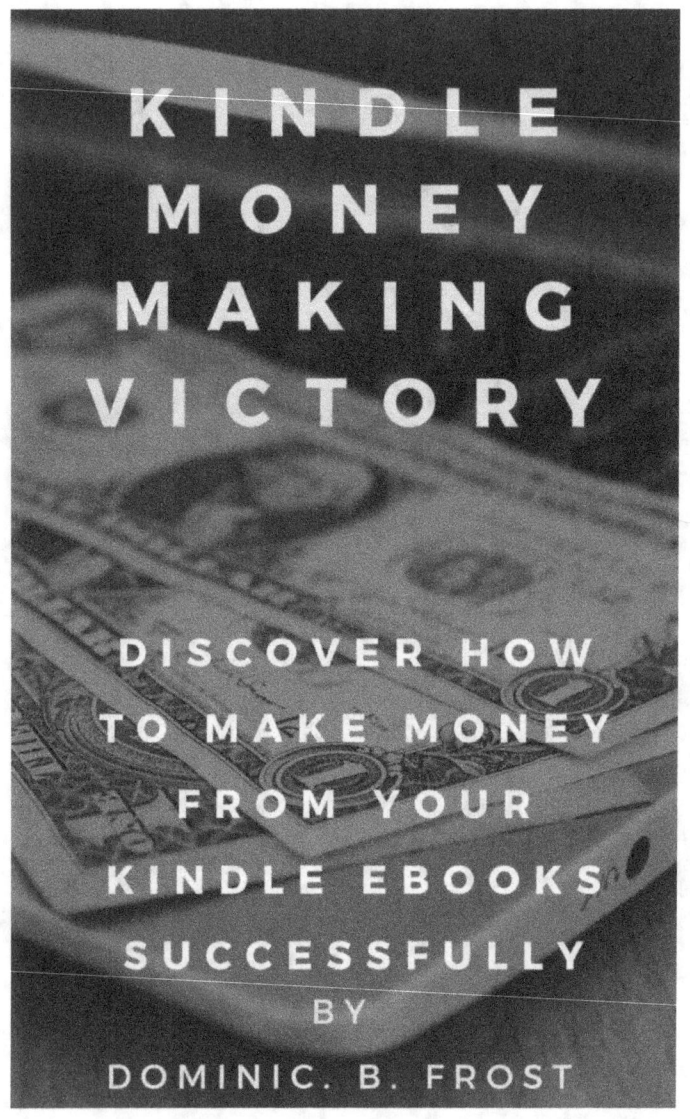

Available To Buy From Amazon At
https://www.amazon.com/dp/B07B7NKS67
Get Your Copy Now

Available To Buy From Amazon At
https://www.amazon.com/dp/B07B7PPYS2
Get Your Copy Now

www.ingramcontent.com/pod-product-compliance
Lightning Source LLC
Chambersburg PA
CBHW030058230526
45471CB00003B/1153